With gratitude to the ancestors and our nonhuman
relatives whose stories remind us where we come from
—D.W., S.Y.S., S.G., J.C.

For my family, who let me see the world for myself
—D.MBD.

Acknowledgments: Many thanks to Jordyn Taylor for her comments on early stages of this
manuscript, to Teresa R. Peterson for advising on Dakota language and orthography, and to
Dr. Malika Kraamer for her expertise on West African clothing.

Carolrhoda Books®
An imprint of Lerner Publishing Group, Inc.
241 First Avenue North
Minneapolis, MN 55401 USA

For reading levels and more information, look up this title at www.lernerbooks.com.

Designed by Viet Chu.
Main body text set in Zemke Hand ITC Std.
Typeface provided by International Typeface Corp.
The illustrations in this book were created with Procreate on iPad.

Library of Congress Cataloging-in-Publication Data

Names: Wilson, Diane, 1954– author. | Shin, Sun Yung, author. | Gibney, Shannon, author. |
    Coy, John, 1958–author. | MBD, Dion, illustrator.
Title: Where we come from / Diane Wilson, Sun Yung Shin, Shannon Gibney, John Coy ;
    illustrated by Dion MBD.
Description: Minneapolis : Carolrhoda Books, [2022] | Includes bibliographical references. |
    Audience: Ages 5–10. | Audience: Grades 2–3. | Summary: "In this unique collaboration,
    four authors lyrically explore where they each come from—literally and metaphorically.
    Richly layered illustrations connect past and present in this accessible and visually
    striking look at history, family, and identity" —Provided by publisher.
Identifiers: LCCN 2021053503 (print) | LCCN 2021053504 (ebook) | ISBN 9781541596122
    (library binding) | ISBN 9781728460765 (ebook)
Subjects: LCSH: Children's poetry, American. | LCGFT: Autobiographical poetry.
Classification: LCC PS3623.I5783 W47 2022 (print) | LCC PS3623.I5783 (ebook) |
    DDC 811/.6—dc23/eng/20220120

LC record available at https://lccn.loc.gov/2021053503
LC ebook record available at https://lccn.loc.gov/2021053504

Manufactured in the United States of America
1-47628-48109-4/8/2022

WHERE WE COME FROM

DIANE WILSON SUN YUNG SHIN SHANNON GIBNEY JOHN COY

ILLUSTRATED BY DION MBD

Carolrhoda Books

Minneapolis

We come from stardust,
our bodies made of ancient elements.

We come from single cells
evolving over billions of years
as did all life on Earth—
bacteria, trees, animals!

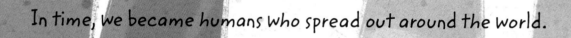

In time, we became humans who spread out around the world.

We come from place, language, and spirit. And each of us comes from story.

I come from Mní Sota Makhóčhe,
a land of forests and clear lakes
where cornfields remember
a vast prairie, a sea of tall grass
home to bison, burrowing owls,
and Dakhóta skipper butterflies.

I come from Korea—green mountains,
black rocks, and cold springs,
wet moss, giant frogs,
and pine trees winding around shadows.

A city grown by the river. That's where I come from.

Named for the stands of bur oak trees,
this city called Ann Arbor is mine.
Our stately old train station downtown sits
not far from an arboretum with iris
and peony gardens that spill into fern walks.

I come from the North,
wind-whipped, snowy afternoons,
when dark comes early,
from Minneapolis, a combination
of Dakhóta and Greek words,
waterfall city on the great river, Mississippi.

I come from hitúŋkakaŋpi, old stories
told in winter by the fire, passed down
from countless generations.

Uŋktómi the trickster helps us remember
what the elders teach: to be Dakhóta,
you must be a good relative.

I come from a long line of dark-haired women
who washed rice,
    spun silk,
        and wrote poems.

I come from stones and trees with spirits,
    Buddhist temples in the woods,
        nine-tailed fox folktales,
        tigers, and red-crowned cranes.

I come from people traveling,
stories from two continents.
One group in Ireland, the other somewhere in West Africa,
planting and harvesting parsnips and barley,
yam and okra.

I come from the animals,
bear, boar, elk, and deer,
who kept us alive long ago in Ireland and Scotland.

I come from groves in the forest—
bounty of nuts, berries, and mushrooms—
and from standing stones, sacred spots for ceremonies.

I come from the breath of plants,
the sweet sap of trees, roasted corn,
first medicine water, parched wild rice,
bison meat sizzling fat on hot coals—
gifts from the land.

I come from five thousand years of a people,
kingdoms that rose and fell, an empire,
movable metal type, and a native alphabet
created so all the people could read and write.

White people called my ancestors "slaves,"
dragging us to this country by force.
We worked on enormous cotton plantations
they thought they owned too.
But the flourishing forests we runaways hid in
also resisted.

I come from Gaelic speakers,
sitting in a wide circle
of stories, myths, and poetry.

I come from a drum, the bodhrán,
and bagpipes, flutes, and fiddles,
songs sung at the céilí deep into the night.

I come from a war in 1862
that forced us from our homeland,
from the bones of our relatives,
from the plants we knew.

I come from grandparents
forbidden to speak their language,
ancestors forced to learn English
at boarding schools.

I come from over one hundred years
of migration across the Pacific,
first on the S.S. Gaelic
to sugarcane plantations and pineapple farms in Hawai'i.

I come from Black folks in Mississippi
who loved the land but
had to leave it behind to stand up,
to find enough space
for we who were coming.

They journeyed to industrial cities in the North,
crowding into tenement houses,
working in factories and meat-packing plants.
All so the babies could finally reach and grow.

I come from the soil,
potatoes planted each year
until blight and famine forced families to flee.

I come from ocean crossings,
Cork to New York, Glasgow to Halifax,
people packed in boats, praying for passage.

I come from my grandmother's garden, picking berries warm from the sun.
My ancestors' prayers brought us home to the land where we have always lived.
Now families dance at powwows, learn our language,
and listen to the old stories once again.

I come from the Chicago skyline,
chasing glowing fireflies at dusk,
borrowing stacks of books from the neighborhood library,
and reading them by flashlight at night.

I come from backyard snow forts
and snowball fights in the park,
from sleepovers in the treehouse,
and s'mores in the firepit.

From parents who love each other,
but sometimes fight
and brothers who never back down
from a dare.

I come from baseball diamonds,
playground basketball courts,
weekly library visits,

and cross-country road trips,
looking to the future,
learning from the past.

We all come from stardust,
sparks of light connected by story,
creating a circle of past, present, and future,
ancestors, families, and you.

What do the stars, the fields, and the rivers sing to you?
What stories does the wind whisper in your ear?

More about Where We Come From

We come from stardust

Yes, this is true. Nearly all the elements in our bodies are made up of atoms that came from stars that exploded billions of years ago. In addition, Dakhóta people are called Wičháŋȟpi Oyáte, Star People, whose spirits came from the Creator along the "spirit road" known as the Milky Way. They emerged at Bdoté, the confluence of the Minnesota and Mississippi Rivers. Both modern science and Dakhóta stories agree that we come from stardust.

We come from single cells

All life on Earth today evolved from single-celled organisms that first emerged roughly 3.5 billion years ago. In fact, bacteria once ruled the whole planet. When bacteria living in oceans began to convert carbon dioxide and water into sugars using energy from the sun—a process known as photosynthesis—they also produced oxygen. This created an atmosphere that allowed many new forms of life to evolve and thrive. Today, bacteria continue to play a vital role in shaping our world, from supporting our immune systems to helping plants grow bigger by providing access to nitrogen.

In time, we became humans

Over millions of years, human ancestors evolved, becoming *Homo sapiens* between two hundred thousand and three hundred thousand years ago. From what is now Africa, humans spread out throughout the world.

I come from Mní Sota Makhóčhe

DIANE: Long before European settlers came to Minnesota, this area was and still is the homeland for Dakhóta people, a Native American tribe. The Dakhóta name for this land is Mní Sota Makhóčhe, which means "the land where the waters reflect the clouds." Just two hundred years ago, much of southern Mní Sota Makhóčhe was covered with a tallgrass prairie that was home to over two hundred different species. This is the land where my mother's family originally came from.

I come from Korea—green mountains

SUN YUNG: Mountains make up 70 percent of the Korean peninsula, with the highest being 백두산 Baekdu Mountain, which stands at 9,003 feet (2,744 m).

A city grown by the river. That's where I come from.

SHANNON: I was born and raised in Ann Arbor, Michigan, a small city by the Huron River founded in 1824. It quickly became the site of the University of Michigan, as well as a prominent stop on the Michigan Central Railroad. But those who founded Ann Arbor were not the first to live here: people from the Wyandot, Odawa, Potawatomi, and Ojibwe Nations were in the area for hundreds of years before this.

I come from the North . . . from Minneapolis

JOHN: Minneapolis is a mistranslation of the Dakhóta word for waterfall and the Greek word "polis" for city. Mississippi means "great river" in Ojibwe and is also known as Ḣaḣa Wakpá, "river of the falls," in Dakhóta. Minneapolis is the site of the only major waterfall on the Mississippi.

I come from hitúŋkakaŋpi, old stories

DIANE: Stories have always been important to Dakhóta people, who used them to record their history and teach values to children as well as to entertain. The hitúŋkakaŋpi often tell about spirit beings, such as Uŋktómi the trickster, whose unruly behavior was used as an example of what children should not do. The Dakhóta believe it is essential to be a good relative to one another as well as all other beings.

I come from a myth

SUN YUNG: The origin myth of Korea includes the King of Heaven, his son 단군 Dangun, a bear, a tiger, an herb called mugwort, garlic, a cave, and other elements.

I come from people traveling

SHANNON: My birth mother was Irish American and my birth father was African American, so I identify as a mixed Black woman. About 4.5 million Irish people came to the United States between 1820 and 1930, fleeing social and economic hardships. My African ancestors, probably from its western coast, likely lived in small villages as farmers, cattle herders, or hunters and foragers.

I come from the animals . . . standing stones

JOHN: My ancestors in what is now Ireland and Scotland relied heavily on food foraged in the forest as well as animals they hunted for meat, clothing, and tools. Standing stones are groupings of enormous stones, often placed in a circle, that have been gathering places for thousands of years.

I come from the breath of plants . . . first medicine

DIANE: Plants use the life-giving process of photosynthesis to transform light, carbon dioxide, and water into food as well as oxygen for humans and animals to breathe. Without photosynthesis, most life on Earth would disappear. Water is called "first medicine" because it gives life.

I come from five thousand years of a people . . . a native alphabet

SUN YUNG: This is a traditional accounting of the continuity of Korean culture, with clans, animism (the belief that everything has a spirit), and pottery, dating to approximately 3000 BCE. 한글 Hangeul is the official language writing system of Korea, and it originated with King Sejong the Great in 1443 during the Joseon dynasty. The Korean alphabet was designed so that everyday people could learn to read and write.

White people called my ancestors "slaves"

SHANNON: Africans were stolen by European merchants and the African elites who forced them to work rice, sugar, cotton, and other plantations in the Caribbean and Brazil, predominantly. While my ancestors were brought to North America, this was not the destination for the majority of enslaved Africans. Of the roughly 10.7 million Africans who made the treacherous journey across the Atlantic on slave ships, fewer than 400,000 were taken to North America.

From Irish and Gaelic speakers

JOHN: Gaelic was the language of Scotland for over one thousand years until it was outlawed in 1616 by English conquerors. In Ireland, Irish was banned by the English in 1695. Both languages continue to be spoken today. A céilí, or cèilidh, which translates as "visit," involves coming together to share old stories, myths, poetry, and songs.

I come from a war in 1862 . . . boarding schools

DIANE: Through several treaties signed in the 1850s, the Dakhóta surrendered much of their land to live on a small reservation along the Minnesota River. After the Dakhóta-US War erupted in 1862, the Dakhóta were forced to leave Mní Sota Makhóčhe.

Beginning in 1879, Native American children were often sent to boarding schools where they were forbidden to speak their language or practice their own spirituality. My mother grew up in a boarding school on the Pine Ridge Reservation in South Dakota. Boarding schools are one of the reasons why so few Native people speak their own languages today. As language is an important part of culture, many Native families are now relearning their Native languages.

I come from over one hundred years

SUN YUNG: On January 16, 1893, United States troops invaded Hawai'i, and the next day Queen Lili'uokalani, under protest, made a conditional surrender of her authority. In January of 1903, as part of ongoing labor immigration to this colony, 102 Korean immigrants arrived in Hawai'i on the S.S. *Gaelic*. The ship brought twenty-one women, twenty-five children, and the rest were "able bodied men." Hawai'i became the fiftieth US state on August 21, 1959.

I come from Black folks in Mississippi

SHANNON: My family was based in rural Mississippi, but like many African Americans, they came north for job opportunities and to flee racist Jim Crow laws. This movement of people, known as the Great Migration, took place between 1916 and 1970 when more than six million Black Americans left the South for the North and West. They completely reshaped the country's economy, culture, and politics in the process.

I come from the soil . . . from ocean crossings

JOHN: The population of northern Europe grew dramatically after potatoes were introduced from South America in the mid-1500s. People in Ireland were particularly dependent on the potato for food, and when blight, a fungal disease, appeared in 1845, it wiped out much of the crop. Over one million Irish people died in the subsequent famine.

Millions of people left Ireland and Scotland in the 1800s on crowded, disease-ridden ships. My Irish ancestors immigrated to the United States, and my Scottish ancestors went first to Canada before coming to the United States. The experiences of leaving home and making the perilous ocean crossing were so difficult that many families did not talk about it. Consequently, I do not know exactly where my Irish and Scottish ancestors came from. This story is a combination of questions, family history, research, and imagination.

I come from the Chicago skyline

SUN YUNG: Intercountry Korean adoption from South Korea to the United States began in 1955. I was adopted from Seoul, South Korea, and grew up in a suburb of Chicago. We lived near my adoptive parents' large extended families, who lived on the South Side of Chicago and elsewhere.

I come from backyard snow forts

SHANNON: My brothers and cousins and I could spend hours building snow forts during cold midwestern winters, treehouses and campouts in other seasons. We were lucky that we had space, active imaginations, and one another.

Pronunciations

bodhrán: BAU-rawn

céilí: KAY-lee

hitúŋkakaŋpi: he-too-ga-gah-pee. In Dakhóta, the ŋ is pronounced like the *ng* in *song*.

Mní Sota Makhóčhe: mNEE so-tuh mah-KO-cheh

Uŋktómi: ook-TO-mee

Where Do You Come From?

"Where are you from?" is a question that some Americans get asked more than others. Sometimes it is a question that can cause children to feel as though they don't belong, which can be hurtful, even when no harm is intended.

The four of us have very different backgrounds and family histories, and yet, as human beings in this universe, galaxy, on this planet, on this continent, in this moment, we have so much more in common. Knowing more about where we come from in terms of land, water, places, peoples, and stories helps us appreciate the beauty and sacredness of how we're related.

Many of us have gaps large and small in our family histories, and that's also part of the larger human story, which unfortunately includes invasions, wars, conflicts, enslavement of one group by another, oppression, and disappearances.

Despite all of the struggles, each of us alive today is part of lineages that have, through a combination of determination and luck, survived. All of human history holds violence and brutality but also times of peace, abundance, and incalculable and unrecorded moments of cooperation, sharing, helping, caring, and adapting to change—otherwise, we wouldn't be here at all.

Our stories are about our own experiences and the experiences of those who came before us, our distant and recent ancestors. Each child's story is priceless, but to shine its fullest, it must be shared, because we are in this life and on this one green-and-blue planet together.

We hope this book inspires readers to feel both unique and part of a big community, and to respect all life and those that came before and those that will come after, because we, with the trees and rivers and rocks and nonhuman animals, are all relatives.

Further Reading

Curtis, Christopher Paul. *The Journey of Little Charlie*. New York: Scholastic, 2018.

Fox, Karen C. *Older Than the Stars*. Illustrated by Nancy Davis. Watertown, MA: Charlesbridge, 2010.

Paek, Min. *Aekyung's Dream*. San Francisco: Children's Book Press, 1978.

Paul, Miranda. *Beyond: Discoveries from the Outer Reaches of Space*. Illustrated by Sija Hong. Minneapolis: Millbrook Press, 2021.

Woodson, Jacqueline. *This Is the Rope: A Story of the Great Migration*. Illustrated by James Ransome. New York: Nancy Paulsen Books, 2013.

Selected Bibliography

Ignatiev, Noel. *How the Irish Became White*. New York: Routledge, 2009.

Murphy, Nora. *White Birch, Red Hawthorn: A Memoir*. Minneapolis: University of Minnesota Press, 2017.

Patterson, Wayne. *The Ilse: First-Generation Korean Immigrants in Hawai'i, 1903–1973*. Honolulu: University of Hawai'i Press, 2000.

Trenka, Jane, Julia Chinyere Oparah, and Sun Yung Shin. *Outsiders Within: Writing on Transracial Adoption*. Minneapolis: University of Minnesota Press, 2021.

Westerman, Gwen, and Bruce White. *Mni Sota Makoce: The Land of the Dakota*. Saint Paul: Minnesota Historical Society Press, 2012.

Wilkerson, Isabel. *The Warmth of Other Suns*. New York: Vintage Books, 2014.